Wakefield Press

a brief letter to the sea about a couple of things

*It's shite being Scottish*, so the *Trainspotting* line goes. And for a long time Ali Whitelock thought that too. Originally from Glasgow, she now lives an hour south of Sydney. Sure, she lives a fortunate life. Sure, the sun shines just about every day. Sure, the beach is only a ten-minute stroll away. So why then is this not enough for her? What is it that makes her heart ache for the Scottish wilds, the icy north wind, the horizontal rain, the Cairngorms, the Old Man of Storr, the best Indian food you will ever taste in your life, and supermarkets that reduce packs of twelve croissants to 5p at the end of the day? Sadly, she has yet to come up with a definitive answer.

Ali spends her days writing, mentoring, applying SPF 50+, looking for her sun hat, fantasising about living in a windswept cottage in winter on the Isle of Skye, and shouting at the telly when the Liberals come on.

*a brief letter to the sea about a couple of things* is her fourth book.

praise for ali whitelock's
*and my heart crumples like a coke can*

'This is brilliant. Funny, heartbreaking and a bit wonky.
Now my internal monologue sounds like an Ali
Whitelock poem (except not as good).'
Graeme Macrae Burnet, *His Bloody Project*, *Case Study*

'Whitelock's gifts to poetry are many. These include showing
how poetry doesn't have to be written for a minority
in order to be first-rate.'
*Saturday Paper*

'Ali Whitelock writes a poetry of excoriating tenderness.
Whitelock is Bukowski with a Glaswegian accent
and a nicer wardrobe.'
Mark Tredinnick, poet & author of *The Blue Plateau*,
*The Little Red Writing Book*, *Blue Wren Cantos*,
*The Lyre Bird & Other Poems*

'In these times when antipodean poetry is dominated
by stay-in-line competition poets I find this collection by Ali
Whitelock honest, invigorating and refreshing. I'm putting this
book right on my top shelf of favourite poetry
published in Australia.'
Dr Brentley Frazer, *Bareknuckle Poets Journal of Letters*

'I didn't even want to review Whitelock, I just wanted
to turn back to the first page and start reading again.'
Simon Sweetman, *Off the Tracks*

# a brief letter to the sea about a couple of things

## ali whitelock

Wakefield
Press

Wakefield Press
16 Rose Street
Mile End
South Australia 5031
www.wakefieldpress.com.au

First published 2023

Cover designed by Stacey Zass
Edited by Julia Beaven, Wakefield Press
Typeset by Michael Deves, Wakefield Press

ISBN 978 1 74305 972 2

NATIONAL
LIBRARY
OF AUSTRALIA

A catalogue record for this
book is available from the
National Library of Australia

CORIOLE
McLAREN VALE

Wakefield Press thanks
Coriole Vineyards for
continued support

*For Karen*

The following poems were part of the Shadow Catchers exhibition at AGNSW, 2020:

'the ophthalmologist instructs my husband', commissioned by Red Room Poetry & the Art Gallery of NSW in response to the photograph *Romance in Granada – The Blind* by Sophie Calle

'& the angel of the lord appeared to him & said to him, "the lord is with you, O mighty man of valour." [judges 6:12]', commissioned by Red Room Poetry & the Art Gallery of NSW in response to the photograph *Yvonne, student, Yugoslavia* by Merilyn Fairskye

'i leaned my head against yours', commissioned by Red Room Poetry and the Art Gallery of NSW in response to the photograph *Untitled (Denise and Diane twinning)* 2018, by Emma Phillips.

# contents

This book would not be possible without the generous support of the arts council of … just kidding. Despite trying, I have never (as yet) been lucky enough to score funding, therefore *all* of my gratitude goes to my husband Thomas, who keeps us both afloat in this blow-up dinghy we call life.

*Dear Reader,*

As our legs buckle under the biggest pile of shite god ever shat out, some say poetry is the answer. Granted, it's mostly poets hoping to sell books who say that. But, look, I'm a poet and lately, what with the world the way it is, even I'm no longer sure that poetry can *always* salve what ails. Our lives have become/were always (?) complicated and multi-layered and if I know anything it's that sometimes there are no simple answers to *things*. That sometimes *things* just *are*. In the same way that poems just *are*. But that doesn't stop me from writing them nor reading them because when I do that, something of me is preserved.

I hide and I find myself in poetry and somehow the six o'clock news kills me a little less. So if you should find a poem in this collection that speaks to you, that it somehow salves what ails, please feel free to hail it as the *Great Betadine of the Grazed Chambers of our Exhausted Hearts.* Or if you are unimpressed by their lack of succour, cast them immediately to the flames.

But here's the thing, I have programmed these poems to whisper your name (yes, *yours*) in the middle of the night, in the same way that a family-sized bar of white chocolate and packets of crinkle-cut chips whisper your name from the dark of the pantry when you're trying to reduce your carbs.

So, if you are holding this book in your hands, if you are teetering on the brink of taking it to the cash register and parting with your hard-earned money for yet another poetry collection you are unlikely to read, if you are white knuckled trying to defy your craving for a freshly baked rhubarb and pear danish, I hope you find yourself powerless to resist.

*Love, ali xx*

# love in the time of celery

i always imagined my yellow brick road would lead me to a future, if not emerald, at least the colour of pale celery. over time the rich yolk of my bricks faded & turned to what dulux might call *malnourished eggshell*. i met & married a migrant who cleaned bricks for a living, fifty dollars for every thousand bricks cleaned, sometimes he'd bring home a couple & keep them on his desk. i was too much of a cunt to see what it was he was really trying to say. he came to this country with no *inglés, pas d'anglais, ich spreche kein englisch*. with time he taught me how to be kind in three different languages. through him i discovered the heart of a shrimp is located in its head, that otters hold hands to stop drifting apart in the sea, that cows produce the most milk listening to REM's *everybody hurts*. after months teaching himself english he got a new job cleaning out stables. when they asked how much english he could speak he oozed his answer with all the ripeness of a french camembert, *not zo much*, he said, *but ze horseez also zay are not speakeeng ze eeenglish eizer.* after the stables he got a job cooking in a french restaurant when it was still compulsory to smoke in the kitchen. at home he continued to keep two bricks on his desk at all times. eventually he gave in to my nagging to replace them with an objet d'art that matched the curtains & pleased *me* more. we went shopping & bought some thing from a shop that meant no thing—a statue of a woman wearing a crown, the torch in her right hand casting shadows that turned the room the colour of malnourished eggshell. *give me your tired,* she seemed to say, *your shrimps & your curtains. give me your bricks, yearning to breathe free.*

# the town itself, let us admit, is ugly

—from Albert Camus' *The Plague*

lunchtime. day 347. i slice my fish thin, fry it in crisco. it comes out a little dry though perfectly edible. i do not take a photo do not post it on instagram i have never baked my own sourdough bread. the man who drives the grocery truck will bring new fish in three days along with the kleen-o-pine, hand sanitiser, toilet rolls—assuming there is no current reenactment of culloden in aisle nine. in the old days we rubbed newspaper together to make it soft, hung the fragile sheets on a nail poking out of the toilet wall. when we came out of the toilet, mum's *bend over so i can read the headlines* never grew old. but who has newspaper at home these days? an ipad streaming the news in HD cannot be used for anything other than reading the news in HD. now mum's stuck in scotland while i'm in australia and qantas regret to announce there are no available flights at this time please check again later. mum says she's worried we won't meet again. i tell her *of course we'll meet again*. now spotify's bombarding me with vera lynn. in japan they sold more copies of *the plague* in one month than the past thirty-one years combined, i mean who'd want to read a book about a plague during an *actual* plague? when my copy arrived i masked up, sanitised the package, peeled off the final frontier in its plastic defence. to be honest i found the story slower than the meserve glacier, duller than the last flicker of the imaginary candle i refuse to hold to it—am i even allowed to say that? few of us dare to be honest these days because, you know, cancel culture. i got one third the way through camus' open-quotes close-quotes masterpiece & tossed it aside in favour of the crown on netflix which i always said i'd never watch but you get so bored. i liked season three better than season four. i ended up feeling sorry for charles. i only mention the fish now because in the old days i ate so little you see. in the slow moving coup of this new-normal it's my head that rumbles with hunger while my days blacken like sliced avocado oxidising on the chopping board of my existence & cravings i cannot satisfy stagger like my drunk father through the deserted streets in the deprived council estate of my mind. but it is not all doom & gloom. for example, my dietary intake of animal protein has increased exponentially. it is an achievement of sorts. if the vaccine under delivers there is comfort in knowing i may end this life with increased muscle mass, less brittle nails—perhaps even the thick luscious hair of my dreams.

**& the angel of the lord appeared to him & said to him, 'the lord is with you, O mighty man of valour.'** [judges 6:12]

her eyes look blootered* / swollen like the plums
that were not in the ice box / but knee-deep by the
river rotting in torrential scottish rain / they were
bruised & slimy / burst & oozing / he was probably
saving them for breakfast /

Question
*what do you tell a woman with two black eyes?*

Answer
*nothing, you already told her twice\*\**

the photo of my parents on their wedding
day is torn in half / held together by the twenty
four hour emergency plumbing magnet stuck to
the door of my westinghouse where i hang all
memories requiring refrigeration / in my

father's half he looks like a boy in a hired
evening suit / his brylcreemed hair peaking to
attention like the great wave off kanagawa / his
legs are spread hands clasped ring finger sporting
the knuckle duster he would cherish from that day
forward for richer, for poorer, in sickness & in-
creasing sickness /

in her torn half she stands meek / stiff
as the plastic bride perched on top of their
3-tier wedding cake / her stilettos sunk
so deep into the icing they have reached
the marzipan /

in the years that followed she would obey
& forsake / take the hammer & smash the
ring with which she he wed / walk into endless
doors / set fire to her white lace dress / swallow
the tut tuts from the good women in line at the
bakery / each teetering precariously on the fragile
shells of their own hypocritical meringues
whispering, *look at the bruises would you …*
*why in god's name does she stay?*

---

* blooter, blouter, bluiter n. and v. [ˈblʌutər, ˈblutər]
—to obliterate, strike excessively hard [often refers to a football]

** In 2020, this still passes as a joke.
source: http://kickasshumor.com/funny-joke/403/
what-do-you-tell-a-woman-with-two-black-eyes-

# the difficulty with honesty in the long-term relationship & the consequences thereof

he had an eye appointment in the city later that day. he is legally blind, hates going to his eye appointments more than he hates, say, the synthetic molecules used in italian perfumes. i brought him coffee in bed, tried to wake him by twirling the random eyebrow hairs spiralling from his forehead into a future no one could have predicted. *come on*, i whisper, *time to get up.* he furrows his brow as though he were in pain—morning is not his time. i make encouraging noises, utter soothing sounds, remind him there is coffee. he lifts the cup to his lips & i take the corner of the doona, start to peel it away from his body slowly & carefully as though i were peeling the fragile skin from an overripe banana. *stop!*, he cries, slams his arms down by his sides locking the doona firmly in place around his body, *i want to ask you something. okay*, i say, *so ask me.* so he says, *what will you do when ...* and i thought he was going to say *i'm in the ophthalmologist*, but what he actually said was, *when i die*, & i said, *well it depends, when were you planning on dying?* & he said, *well what if it was next week?* & i said, *well, i'm not really sure when do you need to know by?* then the mood changed, the duvet got tossed off the bed & landed like a soft parachute on the carpet. later i found him in the bathroom naked with his back to me bent over peering into my 7x magnifying makeup mirror. i put my arms around him looked over his shoulder into the reflection of his magnified eyes. *do you ever think you made a mistake marrying me?* he asked. then i said, *is this another trick question?* and he said, *no, it's a serious question requiring a serious answer.* so i said, *well, when do you need to know by?* then the door got slammed & i was left peering into my own magnified eyes.

# geschwindigkeitsbeschränkung. it is not the longest word in the german language

i would tell you of my qualifications, but really i've none to speak of. but i do know stuff, some of it interesting—like why drystane dykes don't fall over, what it means when fresian cows lie down in the field, what mum means when she rubs her hands briskly together on a freezing november morning & says, *by christ, there's snaw ahint it!* i can speak french quite fluently & twenty-nine words of german one of which is *geschwindigkeitsbeschränkung.* it is not the longest word in the german language. i have a smattering of spanish which would allow me to confidently order garlic prawns & a cup of white coffee if i were to find myself in, say, madrid or barcelona—& if pushed, could answer IN SPANISH the question, *how many white shirts do you have in your suitcase?* right now i'm in my french phase, married to a parisian born in the sixteenth arrondissement, look it up it's super fucking posh. i speak french willy nilly at home, have french soap at the bathroom sink & jars of baby french cornichons in my pantry—the ones you can only get at certain delis (the super fucking posh ones). my husband likes browsing luxury items on the hermès website & looks longingly at scarves that cost more than a thousand dollars. he keeps threatening to buy me one. i tell him i could buy five hundred for that in the $2 store. i wear my scottish frugality on my sleeve. during my german phase i swept hair from the floor of a salon called *das haar*. *das haar* is german for *the hair*. the uniform was a black jump suit with a zip right up the front. we had to embroider the salon name discreetly onto the front pocket in red. mum said she'd do it for me. when I got to the salon the next day i took the jumpsuit out of my bag to discover mum had embroidered DAS HAAR in massive red block capitals that took up my entire back. i stuffed it back into my bag & told the blonde manager who was a cunt to everyone i'd forgotten to bring my uniform that day. she sent me home. the experience reminded me of the time i played the part of a monkey in the school production of jungle book. mum fashioned a monkey tail from the sleeve of a fake fur coat & sewed it lovingly onto to the arse of my leotard. that night before school i tried it on along with my monkey mask & was excited to see i really did look like a monkey. i couldn't wait to show it off at rehearsal. next morning the entire cast was gathered in the change room. one by one each monkey removed their duffle coat & twirled dramatically, showing off their leotards. mine was the only leotard with a tail sewn onto its arse. i kept my duffle coat on, walked backwards as casually as i could out of that cloakroom, locked myself in a toilet cubicle & wrenched that fucken monkey tail off leaving a hole in my arse the size of a fist. my favourite comedian is bill hicks.

sometimes i wish bill were still alive. i watch his videos over & over—know every one of his sets, word for word. sometimes i say the lines before bill can say them himself then i laugh out loud, even though now i have to force it 'cause there are only so many times you can laugh at the same joke. given i'm still in my french phase i'm watching a lot of french movies. the people at blockbuster treat you differently when you hire a french movie, they don't ask for your membership card, your password, proof of ID, nothing. sometimes they don't even charge you the late fees. no sir, when you hire a french movie at blockbuster, they treat you as if you are a woman of the world & i let them believe whatever it is they need to believe.

# the earth is dead & we have killed her. how shall we comfort ourselves, the murderers of all murderers?

—after Nietzsche

this poem is formal notification that you are in default of your earthly obligations. unless the full amount of moral fibre is paid inside fourteen days of receipt of this poem earth has no choice but to begin formal proceedings against you. sure, we are all Ein Berliner but we are also Ein Dutch Boy with our fingers in a dike bulging with apathy. haven't you heard? god is dead—thoughts & prayers won't help you now. i remember when a collapsing ice shelf meant too many tv dinners stacked in the freezer. the man on the news said it's already happening, we are all in this together the frozen peas of our hope scattering across the linoleum of our despair. & as our cod suffocate & koalas burn try to remember the password to your moral account, download the pdf of your conscience, save it in a folder marked:

*why    didn't    we    do    more?*

& when you have used up the last of what seemed to be good reasons for getting out of bed, take your savings from the repealed carbon tax, buy dead roses from the petrol station flown in last week from Ecuador, display them in jam jars in the windows of your soul, imagine

them glowing like candles lit in the name of saint tony* member for
warringah, feel the weight of their petals

pull

your

faded

pink

sad-

ness

to

the

sill.

*tony abbott is a liberal ex-prime minister of australia & former member for
the electorate of warringah who publicly stated that 'climate change is crap'
& who, upon election, repealed the carbon tax implemented by the previous
labor government. prior to politics abbott briefly trained as a roman catholic
seminarian.

# the *not-that-interesting-to-some* story of the thin brown cleaner on the student visa

this is the cafe in the yoga studio in the posh end of town where i used to live when it was still okay to have more than one belly, tree trunk thighs & turmeric lattes weren't even a thing.

this is the cafe where the painfully thin, fake tanned, overly made-up women gather before yoga to nibble on gluten-free bliss balls, only ever eat plant-based diets, breathe organic air & talk about vegan-this, gluten-free-that, fucking lactose-free the next thing.

this is the shop across the road called lulu lemon where the painfully thin women buy their lycra tops & fluorescent leggings that allow them to go much deeper into downward dog than if they wore a t-shirt & tracky dacks from say, target or kmart.

this is the cafe in the yoga studio where the painfully thin women eat things that resemble cakes but have no cake-like ingredients & taste like fermenting weeds & decomposing cabbage & are topped with a single fresh flower to fool you into thinking you are about to eat something good.

this is the cafe where the painfully thin women do not merely drink, but hydrate with hibiscus kombucha & cinnamon-infused water before they enter the yoga studio which is heated to forty-two degrees because they want to know what it feels like to suffer as painfully thin brown people suffer on hot continents far away in villages without electricity & clean drinking water.

just kidding. this is the yoga studio where the painfully thin women enter the forty-two-degree room in order to hold their poses till the contents of their lymphatic systems drain onto the floorboards & there is a very bad smell.

oh look, here comes the painfully thin brown cleaner who smiles at the painfully thin women who are too busy hydrating to smile back at him.

the same thin brown cleaner on the student visa which restricts the number of hours he can work; where the private college he's studying the advanced diploma of business charges him like a wounded bull; who drinks un-infused water from the tap; eats whatever is available & who, despite working two jobs & studying full-time still manages to rise at dawn, salute his own internal sun & go deep into downward dog in a loose t-shirt & tracky dacks from say, target or kmart.

oh look, here on the coffee machine is the young
italian man called otto who is also on a student visa
& has trouble with english & fucks up every order
he ever takes but has a perfectly sculpted jawline,
wears tight fitting t-shirts, smiles his charming
smile, says *bongiorno* & *ciao bella* to the painfully
thin women who smile back at him moon-eyed
while patting down their sweaty hair & pulling the
lycra out of their arse cracks & who do not mind in
the slightest getting an oat milk latte when in fact
they ordered an almond milk cappuccino.

& here is the boss of the yoga studio who instructs
the thin brown cleaner to add the environmentally
friendly, antibacterial, biodegradable liquid to the
mop bucket before mopping up the toxins from
the floorboards in the studio in a way that doesn't
make the bacteria feel bad or unloved or any less
important than say, acidophilus or bifidus.

& here again is the painfully thin brown cleaner
with the vacuum cleaner on his back, quietly doing
as he is told & smiling at the painfully thin women
as they sip on their wrong orders & even though
they do not smile back at him, still he accepts them
with their too much make-up, their fake tans &
their lulu lemons for who they are despite their
gluten & other non-dietary related intolerances.

# a brief letter to the sea about a couple of things

DEAR sea,
you are so very
full. no amount of
hosing the concrete could empty
you. you are also very deep, like our
friend hamish, a doctor of philosophy at
glasgow uni who took the tv remote control
to the supermarket & tried to use it to call home
to find out if they needed milk. dear sea, what *shall*
we do with a drunken sailor, his swollen belly rising &
falling like a tide of rum & cokes ear-ly in the morning? i
like you best at dark when the moon's not full & the car park's
empty. no fishermen casting their lines under a van gogh sky. no
severed ears to hear the stifled screams of my recycled dreams thrown
into the commingled bin. no one to call for the status of milk in my fridge. no
one to notice when i finally drown.

**ur**
**body**
**is**
**60%**
**water**

some
times             from      u
ur      ur      there      here      will      they
body      grief      is      on      pass      will
is      will      no      in      this      wander
60%      be      manhole      nothing      hole      the
water      bigger      lid      will      onto      earth
than      big      comfort      ur      full
the      enough      u      children      of
beached      to                     holes.
whale's      cover
belly      the
u      hole
find      left
urself      in
in      you

# it will start innocently enough with the ovarian cyst

you will be in your forties. you will never have been admitted to hospital before. it will turn out the suspected ovarian cyst will in fact be a tumour.

during surgery they will discover it has engulfed the ovary. the ovary will need to be removed. it will be expensive & inconvenient but there will be minimal pain. post op the doctor will call you with the pathology results & tell you the tumour was borderline malignant. the word malignant in association with any part of your body will freak you the fuck out.

this experience will remind you you are not getting any younger. you will decide to try to fall pregnant. you will be made aware the chance of falling pregnant at this age is less than 5%. this equates to a lot of sex you are not convinced you are prepared to endure. however, in preparation you will stop taking the contraceptive pill you have been taking for the last twenty-odd years. this will bring about the reemergence of the period pain you started taking the pill for. this pain will floor you in ways you do not have words for.

you will tell the gynaecologist of this pain. he will prescribe many pain killers & anti-inflammatories. some will be taken orally & some will be inserted up your arse. surprisingly, the latter will offer the greatest relief. you will unintentionally overuse the anti-inflammatories & fail to take seriously the leaflet advising you to always take with food. as a result your duodenum will perforate & you will end up in hospital with a raging infection in your gut.

while in the emergency department a nurse will feed what feels like a garden hose up your nose & down your throat into your belly to draw out the pooling poison. a further two nurses will be required to hold you down. this will be the most terrifying experience of your life.

when your next period comes around & you cannot speak because the pain is so great your husband will take you in a taxi to the gynaecologist's office to show him precisely how much pain you are in. you will be laid down by the very concerned looking receptionist on the plush velvet sofa in the dimly lit reception area. the walls will be a contemporary dark grey, the room adorned with expensive soft furnishings & what appear to be ming vases.

the gynaecologist will announce on seeing you he had no idea such pain were possible. you can only assume when you previously (& repeatedly) told him of this pain, he had no way of comprehending what this may mean.

he will immediately recommend a complete hysterectomy. you will immediately accept. the hysterectomy will be performed two weeks later & he will leave the second ovary in place after all, why remove a perfectly functioning ovary?

turns out the reason you'd remove a perfectly functioning ovary is because if there was a borderline malignant tumour in the first ovary, there's a chance it will appear in the second.

your new gynaecologist will suggest immediate surgery to remove this 'ticking timebomb'.

the night before surgery she will call to tell you the latest research suggests the appendix is believed to be the primary site of ovarian cancer. while we're in there, let's remove that too.

in the weeks post surgery, you will be plunged into surgically induced menopause. you are 44. at first it will feel hilarious to be hot all the time & you will ask everyone in every room you go into, *is it hot in here or is it just me?* you will discover there is even a book with this title. you will be hot in every room, every day for the next eleven and a half years.

somehow you will get to this point in your life without ever really knowing what scar tissue is. but you will find out when it becomes the cause of your small bowel obstruction which has now come out of 'nowhere'.

you will be trolleyed into x-ray where your blockage will make you projectile vomit repeatedly. the vomit will pool on the linoleum floor & nurses will slip on it. the radiographer will bring a mop for the floor & paper towels soaked in cold water to press gently against your now swollen face. this will bring a comfort that will make you think the radiographer is in fact an angel cunningly disguised in a hospital logo'd polo shirt.

after the x-ray, a nurse will feed another garden hose up your nose & down your throat. you will be more terrified than the first time because this time you will know what is coming. three nurses will be required to hold you down.

the 'What To Expect After A Small Bowel Obstruction' discharge sheet will advise you to always chew your food until it is liquid. the word liquid will be underlined. everything you put in your mouth from here on in will cause you fear.

two years later an abscess will appear in your sigmoid colon. you will be hospitalised repeatedly over the coming twenty-four months for recurrent infections. a decision will be taken to remove forty centimetres of your bowel. by robot. yes, really.

and what will become of this body now with its dwindling organs & scar tissue?

well, this is what will become of it: the muscles in your pelvic floor will start to sag like floorboards in a victorian terrace and your bladder & colon will feel as though they may, at any given moment, fall out through your vagina.

you will now have to exercise your pelvic floor muscles to merely keep your dwindling organs inside of you.

and every night as you squeeze your pelvic floor muscles twelve times & hold for the count of ten you will imagine what's left of your organs clinging to the walls of your abdominal cavity screaming out to each other across the void, *for the love of god, hold on as tightly as you can! if you don't fall out through this black fucking hole she will have you removed. she got rid of the others—she will get rid of you too.*

# my friend says it looks like they just had sex

—after Lucian Freud's painting, *And the Bridegroom*

At the art gallery of NSW, i ask my friend what she thinks Freud's painting is about. she says, *it looks like they just had sex.* i say, *are you crazy? it looks like they've been married for thirty years, there's no fucking way they're still having sex! look at her,* i say, *she's exhausted. look at her hair, dangling off the end of the mattress trying to escape her head. look at her eyes, closed to what she cannot change, accepting what she cannot see. and look at him,* i demand, *legs splayed, the weight of his knee pushing her to the brink where she clings on for reasons even she can't quite understand. at the same time they don't look exactly unhappy together—lonely perhaps, resigned.* i drift off for a moment, stare at Kirchner's *Three Bathers* hanging on the wall opposite. *& another thing,* i say, turning back to the Freud, *look at the disgrace of the blanket they're lying on—uncomfortable looking thing— creased & lumpy like a canvas tablecloth that needs a good ironing.*

more than once i've stood in front of that painting, imagined taking two corners of the blanket & yanking it as though from under a perfectly set dinner table—ikea wine glasses, plastic salt shakers & two-dollar dinner plates from kmart go flying. she goes flying too. lands on the floorboards, her eyes closed still. he lands on top of her, crushing her like he always does.

# ode to the french man with the big nose i dated when really i should have known better

first there was your trench coat                    then  your
oversized nose        then your egg-shaped head that rose
up through your bald patch like mount kosciuscko rising
up through the clouds      you   reminded   me   of   inspector
clouseau from the pink panther    side-on   you   looked   like
gainsbourg   & you drank like him        though  you  would
not have known a musical note if it jumped up & bit you on
the arse          i waited on your doorstep that night for three
hours              you brought me french champagne to make
up for it & two crystal flutes you stole from the bar
once indoors you made a toast to the future
soaked the inside tubes of toilet rolls in lighter fuel
        burned them in the kitchen sink for warmth
        then  there  was  the  other  time  you  stole  the  glass
candle holder from the table at la mamma trattoria
you stuffed it inside your trench coat              it dropped
out as we left     the thick glass shattered          still  warm
wax oozed onto the terracotta tiles flown in from milan for the
complete italian experience              people stared
        you laughed          hailed a cab
we went back to your place              you   drank   some
more            the shouting started              the neigh–
bours called the police    they came into the bedroom
        one male one female              the  female  sat  on
the bed beside me              asked about the bruising
        i didn't know what to say.

# ring-a-ring-a-roses

ring-a-ring-a-roses a pocket
full of low self esteem & the
amorous attention of a psycho-
path posing as a Sensitive New
Age Guy but who is actually a Caring
Understanding Nineties Type

      atishoo!

          atishoo!

              i

        so

      fucking

                    literally
     fell

        right

           down.

# vodka & coke

winter. the sea is visible from every room of the air bnb. this is the view you paid for along with the eye-watering cleaning fee & additional service charge you were not expecting. the host meets you at the agreed hour tells you where to put your rubbish what time to check out to be respectful of his neighbours. you speed read the house rules unpack your sadness empty your boot stacked with vodka, like a cargo ship planning on being at sea forever. let the soft clink of bottle comfort you like the conversations you used to have when you still had friends. pour yourself a shot—yes it is breakfast time, vodka goes with everything. float to the beach. sit down on the sand do not be afraid, it will not swallow you. let the soft poultice of your lungs draw the marrow from the bones of the sea. allow your floodgates to open. invite the waves in, there is nothing to fear. feel the corner of your heart lift & rise like the old carpet in the garage that night of the flood. do not worry about your arrhythmia your heart will sync to the certainty of the waves. roll up your jeans, paddle in gently but do not wade too deep it is still too soon. feel the wind whip your hair into stiff peaks of salted meringue. keep your eye on the weather. the lighthouse keeper is dead there is no one to keep us safe any more. trail as much sand as you like back to the air bnb, the host will not be pleased but this is not about him. when the darkness has sucked the last dregs of light from your days turn to your cargo. mix your sadness with coke. toss the screw top of your pain onto the pile rising in the corner like mould up the wall of a gorbal's flat

& when your burden is fully
unbuttoned lay your meringue
on the pillow, slip numbly
into the warm throat of your
dreams curl up with the sea
urchins, sing to the starfish,
waltz with the seahorses
sleep
      with
           the
                moon.

# i
# leaned
# my
# head
# against
# yours
[part i]

as though my forehead were a mouth i could
share secrets through. i was never a good person
though somehow i am surrounded by angels.

as children we weren't twins but we dressed
almost the same in clothes mum made from
remnants of bewildered reds, injured blues,
disquieting yellows. too often there was
enough fabric for matching headscarves.
with our monobrows in our grey scottish
swing parks we were the frida kahlos of our time.

when i no longer knew what to do with it i
breathed my secret into your forehead then
careened through the fog of the swing park,
pulled on a punctured life jacket with a red
light & whistle for not attracting attention. in
the shadow of a marooned shopping trolley i
tore the wings off butterflies.
drowned bees in a jar.

# i
# leaned
# my
# head
# against
# yours
[part ii]

in the days before anti-caking agents my
grandmother kept the salt cellar on the hearth,
her blini ingredients behind the fluted glass
doors of the kitchen cabinet. two ceramic
swans swam lazily across her sideboard, their
hollow backs transporting house keys, fisher-
man's friends, silver shillings down the river
to nowhere.

the last time i saw him was
in my dreams—wrapped in
curtains that didn't quite
reach the floor & shuffling
towards a roaring log fire.

i watch on, hoping he'll trip & be engulfed in
flames. instead he pirouettes from the curtains,
turns to face me, his pink fingers fat like pork
sausages spread terrifyingly across the mantelpiece.

i wake thinking of bees.

# i
# leaned
# my
# head
# against
# yours
[part iii]

in the foyer of the blackpool boarding house
we wait while the landlady wipes down her
condiment sets & stores them away behind the
fluted glass doors of her kitchen cabinet. she
shows us to our accommodation. the five of us
sleep in the same room. in the absence of a telly,
my father, itching for a drink & not knowing
what to do in a room full of his own
children, makes sad shadow puppets on the
wall—a one-eared dog, a not-preying-
drowning mantis, a peace dove having
a heart attack mid-air.

the next morning after breakfast we stroll
along the seafront filling our lungs with the
good sea air we're instructed to inhale deeply.
we pause by the amusement arcade with its
shop selling lacklustre starfish, brightly
embarrassed crabs, fragile seahorses that once
danced to the music of the sea. a solitary

shaved coconut transformed into a tiny hand
bag hangs from a hook in the corner, yellow
rapunzel braids dangle off each side. its
womb-like interior lined with warm velvet—a
place to whisper my secrets, to bury the bees
i've yet to drown.

# the ophthalmologist instructs my husband

WE SIT in the dark of the room.
the ophthalmologist instructs my
husband to move his head forward
place his chin here his forehead
there takes her ophthalmoscope &
checks his retina for threatening new
bleeds, his macula for further
degeneration, her keratometer to explore the sudden craters
& soft folds in the parched paddock of his cornea. then
she opens the manilla folder removes the lid of her montblanc
& carefully charts each new contour in the faded ordnance
survey map of my husband's eyes. the ceiling light is turned back
on. our pupils recoil in the fluorescence of its truth. a requiem in
D minor exits the ophthalmologist's
opening & closing mouth one note at a
time like slow cars over a cliff as
my husband's vision is committed to
the ground earth to earth ashes dust
etcetera with no hope of resurrection
to eternal life. the ophthalmologist
advises there'll be a letter to take to
centrelink something about a pension
card cheap travel discount on our
water rates royal blind society
scanners white canes magnifiers
guide dogs concessions at the theatre
two movie tickets for the price of one.
outside rain pools in pavement
drains blocked like tear ducts all beauty
sucked like diesel from the petrol tank
of the world. the sky, black as a
detached retina riddled with blind
spots is strewn with stars that twinkle
like braille spelling out a million
angry messages to
god.

# mum always has loads of brilliant ideas

like the time she suggested i get a cocktail cabinet installed in my alcove & stock it with babychams for those unexpected guests. then the other time she thought about covering my father's entire body in nicotine patches while he slept. & in the morning when she'd find him dead, eyes wide & astonished like he'd smoke a thousand fags in the night, she'd peel the patches from his cold blue skin & dispose of the evidence before calling the police, or whoever it is you call when there's been a death in the night.

—*but what of the hair?* i asked, *of the perfectly bald squares left behind once the patches were removed?*

—*well,* she said, *we'd just have to shave his entire body before the police came to make things look even.*

—*but mum, what of the questions of a perfectly shaved corpse? there'd be suspicion of foul play, a trip to the station, maybe a coroner's enquiry!*

mum agreed we'd have to think things through a bit more thoroughly, just like we did when i got the cocktail cabinet installed in my alcove.

& usually it's mum who has all the brilliant ideas, but that night over a babycham i told mum not to lose heart, that there were other ways—things i'd read about

on the internet like poisons that go undetected &
euthanasia hoods. mum dipped her carrot crudité into
the home-made baba ganoush i'd knocked up the day
before & kept chilled overnight in the cocktail cabinet
in my alcove.

—*do the hoods come in different sizes?* she asked, idly
crunching on her crudité.

—*probably small, medium & large i would have thought,* i
told her.

—*no extra large then?* she said, loading up her carrot with
more baba ganoush & taking a good swig of her perfectly
chilled babycham—*'cause i really think we'd need to go the
extra large. mind you,* she said, still chomping, *even then
it might be snug.*

# grabbing a coke & a pussy with you

if cheeseburgers & kfc & fox & friends in your bathrobe is
your thing then this is a very good president.

against the nuclear glow of his tangerine rind the concealer
under his eyes is fifty shades too white.

in the beginning i felt sorry for melania though my husband
says she's no better than him.

a handwritten sign outside his scottish golf course reads:
*trump is a cunt* & many feel this is an accurate portrayal.

on the eighth of november two thousand & sixteen no one
imagined things could get worse.

in twenty twenty the whitehouse turned out the lights,
erected a fence, called in the national guard.

that same dark night this *not-my-president* inspected his
bunker while i took refuge in mine & prayed for aliens to
abduct me & take me to *their* leader.

i miss my obama tote bag. his amazing grace. how he
steered this country like a corvette on *comedians in cars
getting coffee,* his wrist resting cool on top of the wheel.

then half a million americans had their lives rubbed out &
archived as acceptable margins of error in a statement of
covid profit & loss.

when the statue of liberty looked down at the plywood coffins being lowered into the mass grave she held her head in her hands & didn't know if she could keep lighting the way.

then came the insurrection & now he infects my dreams. last night he was facetiming his bff, xi.

they're eating chocolate cake, sucking on large cokes, trading favourite stories of the times they tear gassed their citizens, sprayed them with rubber bullets, knelt on their necks till they died.

hey xi, trump sprays, you know, grabbing a coke & a piece of delicious chocolate cake with you really is one of my favourite things—after seeing a cop car cut through a crowd of americans like a knife through butter, of course.

xi, did you know (& i'm not talking about the kung flu here) that thirty-seven thousand americans died of the beautiful regular flu last year?

i mean i'm a very stable genius who owned his own university, plus i had an uncle who was a professor & even i didn't know that & i'm someone who has all the facts, the best facts, actually, some say, the most beautiful facts.

one other thing you may not know is that rocket man is a very good leader. a pretty smart cookie. how he had his own beautiful half brother shot like that. the way he starves his people.

speaking of starving, i actually had korean food one time.

i didn't like it.

it came with something call kimmy, kim-ee, kim-cheese, something like that. how come everything in korea is called kim?

hey xi, do you know kim kardashian?

she's actually a very good friend of mine.

& her ex-husband kanye.
beautiful people. really great people. but i didn't eat that kim-cheese stuff.

hey xi, tell me that one again about your perfect chinese tank trundling into Tiananmen square.

have i ever shown you a picture of my daughter?

you know if she wasn't my daughter i'd probably be dating her.

do you have a daughter, xi? when you wrap your arm low around her waist do you ever feel like dating her?

have you ever grabbed a chinese woman by the pussy, xi?

i gotta tell you no one respects women more than i do & i hear there are twenty-five of them accusing me of sexual assault which is amazing to me, 'cause none of them were actually attractive enough for me to be interested in.

i mean, i'm automatically attracted to beautiful, xi. i just start kissing them.

it's like a magnet.

just kiss—grab 'em by the pussy.

i don't even wait.

i know you're not a star like me, xi, but you should definitely try grabbing a chinese woman by the pussy next time you get the chance.

when you're a star, they let you do it.

when you're a star, xi, you can do anything.


*This found poem includes statements made by trump before & while he was in office.

# i am an orange

peeled juiced & quartered at half-time, served
up on a plate to refresh the boys. on the longest
      stretch of my road the gauge on my tank reads
nearly empty with no petrol stations indicated on
      google maps that normally indicates
everything

      everything to refresh the boys, at half-time i am
served up on a plate. there is no juice. the earth a giant
      uterus spins maniacally on her axis bent double
clutching a hot water bottle lunar month after
      lunar month

      lunar month after lunar month the boys are peeled.
i am quartered but not refreshed. there is still a plate.
      on the longest stretches of my uterus i spin maniacally
on the road. my hot water bottle has been peeled my
      juice has been halved. half-time has been quartered

      at half-time there are no quarters. my juiced uterus
is offered up to refresh the boys. the boys are still peeled.
      there are no oranges on the longest stretch of my road.
my tank is empty. the boys spin maniacally
      on a plate.

# his own daughter is ugly too

in the greek coffee shop i perch on the corner
of the wooden bench. the sea is just about
visible if i lean ever so slightly to the left. it is a
deliberate decision i take to sit here on my own
to sip my morning coffee uninterrupted. i call
this space my stent—the quiet place where i try
to clear the blockages which are almost always
of the heart, the quiet place where i ponder
what might want to be written this day though
the truth is sometimes there is nothing much
to write about. this morning the greek coffee
shop owner comes across, cup in hand, pulls up
a chair—they invite themselves in here. it is a
small village, perhaps even a hamlet. then her
son arrives, cup in hand, also pulls up a chair. he
is forty. she tells me he was the ugliest baby she
had ever seen. he merely draws on his fag, nods
acceptingly, adds how his own baby daughter
was ugly too. my dog sits with us. his name is
hector. the greeks tell me i should have called
him achilles for he is majestic—noble & proud
as a trojan prince though he is not the fighting
type. in fact he makes no sound. just lies at
home on his bed in the corner, asks nothing
of me & i swear sometimes you would not even
know he was there. the coffee shop owner tells

me despite being ugly her son was a good baby,
in fact he made no sound, he'd just lie at home
on his bed in the corner, ask nothing of her &
she swore sometimes you would not even know
he was there. then i said he sounds just like
hector—& the words are out before i realise
how they must sound.

# on ramming a sock down earth's throat

look mate, earth exaggerates—like every fucken
woman does. if you ask me, she's asking for a lesson
she won't forget in a hurry. if i hear her banging
on one more time about her rare earth metals &
her orangutans, her rising sea levels & forest fires i
swear i'll ram a sock right down her throat exactly
like alan jones wished our prime minister would
do to Jacinda Ardern. i mean, mate, sure it hasn't
rained for sixty days, but who wants to suck on a
tooheys on the beach in the fucken rain, mate?
that's right, no cunt. hey, earth, try walking a mile
in my plastic moccasins made in china, mate, fuck
you & your soil erosion, what about my human
rights erosion? what about the free plastic bags
we used to get in the supermarket, now somehow
we're to blame 'cause of our iphones & gas guzzlers
& that frankly fucken delicious chocolate spread.
fair fucken dinkum mate, look at her, all hoity
fucken toity like she's the best thing since sliced
bread charred in the Best Bush Fires in the World
2020, mate. i've a good mind to show her who's
boss, mate, let her feel the back of my hand across
her red hot fucken face. i tell you what mate, it's
time she understood it's not all about her.

(except that it is.).

# i make japanese paper cranes in an attempt to be anything other than this

ancient
japanese
legend
promises
anyone who
folds a thousand
origami cranes will
be granted a wish by
the gods. i have folded
two-hundred-&-forty-three.
i am in no rush. in these bereft
days of covid nothing, i am aware
my excessive consumption of green-
tea ice cream, pickled ginger, miso soup
& the vintage kimono hung precariously on
the bamboo pole above my bed won't bring me
closer to the japanese zen i am looking for. still, i
teeter on blocks of wood that don't fit me, bow endlessly
to people i care nothing for. i enjoy sushi but wasabi gives me reflux
                        & nothing will relieve it.

# ode to the twenty-five kilos my husband lost

HE SHED
twenty-five kilos in six months.
a friend we hadn't seen in years came
to visit, noticed his weight. she's always
trying to lose weight herself—juices kale,
eats quinoa, salad greens without dressing,
does yoga—the hot one—& still the kilos
will not shift. she asks him what his
secret is. he tells her the dog died.
how the grief is
eroding him.

# the unbearable lightness of bacon

we
used
to
take
him
to
the
cafe
with
us
every
day. our standing order was one bacon & egg roll + two
flat whites, though we always call them great whites
cause we're in australia & you know, sharks. whenever
the waiter left the kitchen carrying the roll hector's
mona lisa eyes would track every millimetre of its journey
to our table. on its arrival thomas would cut a piece of
the sizzling bacon & leave it at the side of his plate to
cool before dropping it lovingly into hector's waiting
mouth. it took us a long time to get used to going to the
cafe without him. one year on our standing order is still
the same. thomas still cuts a piece of sizzling bacon, still
leaves it to cool at the side of his plate. we both stare at
the bubbles of fat till they stop bubbling. neither of us
says a word. we dare not lock eyes.

# yin & fucking yang

She orders an avocado, spinach & kale smoothie with a scoop of non-dairy yoghurt, tells me she's vegan & a *bit* bi polar, which sounds like being a little bit pregnant or nearly having cancer or teetering on the cusp of greatness. she takes a thick suck on her smoothie while i dunk my croissant in my café au lait, a practice i found disgusting till i read that Madame Verdurin (in that long book Proust wrote) needed to dunk a croissant so badly, she got a migraine if she didn't. i keep dunking, try to look sophisticated—& as though i'm listening intently though truth be told we have nothing much to connect us now apart from the two dead dogs we used to walk on the beach together. i dunk some more, marvel at the layers of soggy pastry falling back into the swimming pool of my coffee. she draws breath from sucking, tells me how each morning she wakes depressed, how when the sun goes down she dies, how bloated clouds make her sad—how she could never live in places like scotland or moscow or scandi-fucking-navia. then the rain came on, how she is out of balance when it rains, how i should have seen her last week totally *in* balance—meditating at dawn, teaching yoga in a room warmed to forty-two degrees, eating organic chia seeds soaked overnight in organic coconut milk with the splash of liquid chlorophyll that makes her feel scraped out & shiny, at one with the great organic goji berry in the sky. then she mentioned god. more than once. then the yin & fucking yang—how hers is out of balance due to having eaten supermarket mung beans when normally she only *ever* buys them from the farmer's market. then she stopped talking & stared glassy eyed into the distance as though she were trying to manifest the perfect future where she'd rise at dawn, knock out a couple of downward dogs & never know the shadow of pain; a future where she'd have a body she didn't despise, love that would last forever, a dog that would never die.

while she was busy manifesting, i riffled through my authentic french market basket & double checked i'd bought everything i needed from the overpriced french providore at the farmer's market:

| | |
|---|---|
| 2 x brie de maux | check |
| 1 x pâté de fois gras | check |
| 2 x crusty baguettes | check |
| 4 x pains au chocolat | check |
| 3 x cans of cassoulet | check |
| 1 x (small) can of snails | check |

1 x (large) bottle of over-
priced lavender laundry
water that makes me feel
i just washed my clothes
in a 200-year-old farm
house in aix en provence        check

it looked like her manifestation might take up
most of the day so i decided to leave her to it.
as i made to leave she opened one eye—not too
wide in case it interfered with her kundalini—
turned towards me, placed the palms of her hands
together, bowed her head & whispered *namaste*.
& i wondered why she was suddenly speaking to
me in a language that wasn't her native tongue,
but i try not to judge, even though i don't always
succeed—hey, i'm well aware we'd all rather
be more exotic versions of who we really are. i
gathered up my overpriced french provisions,
adjusted my beret till it sat alluringly to one side,
leaned across her carbon-neutral-recycled-enviro-
bamboo-BPA-free-compostable cup, said au revoir,
kissed her on both cheeks, & went gladly on my
own delusional, non-genetically modified way.

# our editors have made their selections. yours were not selected

Poetry Editor
Blah Blah 'Literary' Magazine
FU99 WTF

31 December 2021

Dear, ahem, 'Poetry Editor'

**Re: Your email of rejection, 31 December 2021**

Thank you so much for your recent rejection, received into my inbox on this, the last day of the year and a time normally reserved for celebration.

I was aware you would be advising poets on the outcome of their submissions around this time and had taken the liberty of chilling a bottle of Veuve Clicquot for the moment your congratulatory email came through.

I will confess I expected your email to thank me profusely for my submission, but due to the high quality of my work and mediocrity of your magazine, you had taken it upon yourself, as is your duty towards the advancement of literature, to forward my poems to the Nobel Prize Committee.

And it is not merely that you rejected my poems, more the cunty way with which you did: 'Our editors have made their selections. Yours were not selected.' No 'Dear Ali', no 'Thank you for your submission', no 'We look forward to reading more of your work in the future'. There is a book called *How to Win Friends and Influence People*. You may like to read it.

May I remind you that without us poets contributing to your magazine FOR FREE, you would have no fucking magazine. I feel this is an important point. The least you can do is be nice. It won't fucking kill you.

I hope your Global Warming themed issue is a great success, though without my two poems, I find it hard to imagine it will be.

I have copied in my friend who was also rejected by you this morning.

She will be taking things up with the queen.

Yours, most sincerely,

*a.w. poet*

# if the gravy hadn't trickled down the flock wallpaper on the feature wall

the morning is dreich. i linger by the radiator pull the net curtain to the side stare out past the whirly jig & the bird bath, panic momentarily at the sight of your coffin in the back of the hearse. the man from the funeral home makes his way up the path, removes his top hat knocks gently on the door tells us it's time. i pause, gather my heart & my bag off the floor, walk out past your grow bags sprouting half-hearted tomatoes, last year's needleless christmas tree, brittle lavender that didn't stand a chance. i climb into the family car next to your mourner-in-chief, your now sort-of-wife & woman we wished we didn't know & imagine for one ridiculous moment the black bird sitting on the bonnet of the hearse is you.

& it didn't have to be like this—if you'd given up the grouse, stopped fucking whores, taken mum like you promised to the costa del sol; if you'd showered mum with roses, cadbury's milk tray, sent her giant padded birthday cards that tinkled out tunes when you opened them; if you'd bought her a massage voucher instead of a plough, diamonds instead of a cement mixer, if you'd stopped dumping our dogs & cats in suburbs far from home, your funeral power point presentation would be filled with photos of you & *mum* together, smiling, maybe even laughing (ok, so we probably wouldn't include that one of mum coming at you with the bread knife that christmas). but if you hadn't battered down the front door with an axe, thrown your stew at the feature wall, if the gravy hadn't trickled down the flock wallpaper, the diced carrots hadn't landed on the hearth & burnt black till they turned to dust, it would have been mum, your mourner-in-chief, taking her rightful place in the family car with me, instead of following behind in her fiat panda, dressed in her funeral hat & coat to match, hanky in her pocket, window wipers going like the clappers, oversized sunnies on a day without sun.

## / the difficulty in drawing a dead man from memory /

/ this is a picture of my da' / i drew it from memory / apart from the straw boater he has somehow started wearing since he died it is a very good likeness / here is another one / this time he is holding a microphone, his mouth jammed open for all eternity mid phrase / he was a very good singer / his favourite songs were *ave maria* & *there goes my everything* but only when elvis sang them / he used to sing them to mum at parties & when he was drunk which is to say always / yesterday i cut him out of a photograph / glued him to a sheet of lined paper / drew a set of wings on him even i could see were too big / then i took my biro & filled the sky with a thousand black m's hoping for a murmuration of birds / i decoupaged the Massey Ferguson 241 tractor from the *Farmers Weekly* i bought months after he died when i was still looking for a connection to something / glued it halfway up the page somewhere not-quite-heaven & not-quite-earth / i am not much of a drawer but i tried to capture the likeness of the puppy, dead on the kitchen floor / the difficulty in trying to capture a dead man's violence from memory is you are not meant to speak ill of the dead / you are meant to find a way to sketch their better angels / no matter how fleeting their appearance /

# on becoming a hypochondriac

e
v
e
r
y

time my legs stiffen up & my
throat won't swallow & my breath
rears up against the hurdle of my
lungs, i am convinced it is motor
neurone disease even though the
doctor tells me repeatedly it is not
hereditary.

# & when i start laughing

i am the morning. he is the nighttime. we are not so much ships, more deflating dinghies that pass in the night. this morning he wakes early. it sounds like nothing—as though the roots of his depression weren't tangled around his ankles, quick-set cement hadn't filled the cavity of his chest. i bring him coffee. it is the least i can do. he takes a sip. his eyelids creak open. thin sheets of morning light slip in through the slits of his pupils like love letters on airmail paper eager to be read while his eyes, adjusting to the light, shuffle chaotically from side to side like two old men pushing their first trolley around aldi since the deaths of their wives. i ask how he slept. he clears his french throat, *well*, he says, his voice still croaky with sleep, *last night i dreamt you were 'aving an affair wiz some schmuck*, the still-too-fresh pain of his dream settled deep in the tram tracks of his brow. & when i start laughing, it is not because of the dream (this is a recurrent theme for him & with good reason) but the word *schmuck* thrown out from the language centre of the brain of this man who, even when he is merely asking me to pass the salt, sounds like Molière, Beaudelaire & Cyrano de Bergerac combined. *so*, he says, misunderstanding, *you theenk eet eez funny?* i stop laughing. try to explain. tell him the word *schmuck* from his mouth is like Gandhi telling mother-in-law jokes or the Dalai Lama, if he had a daughter, saying if she wasn't his daughter, he'd be dating her. i sit down on his side of the bed, take his hand, wipe the frantic shock of post-dream hair from his cheek. *have you been up half the night watching american movies again?* he nods. his blind eyes sealed shut again like tutankhamun's tomb. i lean in closer till my own tram tracks are embedded in his, *haven't i told you,* i whisper, *nothing good ever comes from watching netflix before bed?*

# a funny thing happened on the way to the supermarket

*eet's nice to live by ze sea* he says in his french
accent as we speed along the coast to the super-
market for our once-a-day legal outing. he works
as an analyst. i write poetry. he challenges me
when I don't think logically. i challenge him
when he doesn't think poetically.

—nice living by the sea? i say. what's nice
     about it?

—*beecauz you can go for ze long walks*
     *along ze beach.*

—& what's so nice about that?

—*beecauz you can see ze horizon & ze sea &*
     *ze sky & ze clouds.*

—i see. & what's so good about that?

—*beecauz eet eez wander-ful being able*
     *to see ze horizon, ze sea, ze sky & ze*
     *clouds!*

—but what's so wander-ful about it?

—*well, eef you live in ze city you cannot see*
     *ze horizon nor ze sea.*

—i get it, but i want more— tell me how it feels
       to see the horizon, the sea, the sky & the
       clouds.

—*ok, so, ze sea makes me happy beecauz eet*
       *is beautiful & blue & it makes ze sloshing*
       *sound.*

—really? is that really the best you can do?
       in case you hadn't noticed,
       i'm       a       fucking       poet
       i need you to tell me how it makes you feel
       to live by *ze sea*. for just one moment i need
       you to forget about Bayesian Theory & the
       Analysis of Competing Hypotheses, to get
       your emotional shovel out & to dig deep.
       i need you to dive headfirst into the well
       of your poetic imagination.

he looks wounded. but tries again.

—*okay, so, how about zees: when i live by ze*
       *sea i can see it morning, noon & night if*
       *i want to.*

—wow, really? that's really what you're giving
       me as your best poetic interpretation? ok,
       so let me help you out a little. how about:

       when i see the horizon, my ribs expand like
       god just gave me mouth to mouth.

when i see the sky, the soft sponge of my
bronchi fill with oxygen exhaled through
the mouths of fucking angels.

when i see the sea, i plunge through
the deepest blue portal of myself.

his eyes twitch in the same way they twitch
when he's in the last phase of building a multi-
factorial model predicting the outcome of a
nuclear submarine's ability to stay undetected
in enemy waters. his smug look tells me he's
getting ready to impress me. i can tell he's
already impressed himself.

—*ok*, he says, clearing his throat in preparation,
　　　　*how about*:

—*ze clouds in ze sky are ze eyebrows of infinity.*

having badgered him to come up with his best
poetic interpretation, i can hardly now tell him
his interpretation is crap. instead i smile, lean
across from the driver's seat, gently squeeze his
knee, half pity, half well-done-for-trying-anyway.
outside, the horizon zips along like a thin stretch

of endlessly chewed sugar-free gum. we make a
right turn, away from the sea—the eyebrows
of infinity, arched & bushy, waggling high
in the afternoon sky.

# at fifty

at fifty, your rose-tinted glasses
mist up with black fly. you (finally)
stop believing in santa claus, the tooth
fairy hangs up her tutu reluctantly hands
in her wand. you now accept at the time of
your demise there will be no angels no harps
no requiem for the dead. by your father's death
bed your will be catapulted (sans helmet) as if
from a great cannon into adulthood. as you fly
through the air, god (?) will thrust a spiral
bound copy of TRANSITIONING TO ADULTHOOD
—A MANUAL FOR WOMEN IN THEIR FIFTIES! into
your hands. put your glasses
on. wipe the black fly off. turn
to page one.

# welcome to transitioning to adulthood —a manual for women in their fifties!

transitioning to adulthood can be a very rewarding time. this is the time in your life when you can, without fear of embarrassment, look however you want & wear whatever you like regardless of what anyone else might think. fuchsia pink lipstick applied outside the lip line? yes, now is the time for that. emerald-green eye shadow applied haphazardly? absolutely! clashing patterns? yes, of course—literally no one  cares! we realise for some women, this empowering new phase in their lives may come earlier but for others, (you), in their fifties and/or during menopause. but whenever you get here, welcome! the following points act as a guide only. many women will experience their transitions to adulthood differently. this manual accepts no responsibility for any adverse side effects not listed here.

SECTION 1

*how will you know you're finally transitioning
to adulthood?*

- you will go back to scotland for a holiday. instead of immersing yourself in the highlands & glamping at loch ness you will unexpectedly find yourself in a hospital having a conversation with the doctor on duty about your father's prognosis. the conversation will take place in a side room. your father will not be present.

- the doctor will advise that once they have conducted their tests there may be a document to sign confirming whether or not, should the situation arise, your father is to be resuscitated. you will wonder why the doctor is even mentioning such a document. your father will die the next morning before the document has been printed & the tests started. you will be holding your father's hand as he dies.

- even though you may not have loved him (in fact he will have spent much of his life being a cunt), it's important to know that sinking feeling engulfing you (which feels a little like your stomach falling out of your arshole) is quite normal. learn to clench your buttocks (& also your vagina, it will strengthen your pelvic floor) & get on with life. we have no other advice to offer on this front.

- there will be a funeral to arrange & a eulogy to read. you will not write the eulogy because you are not prepared to tell lies about what a great person your father was. but you will be saved from this task by your sister who is very good at these things & even once wrote a eulogy in italian for her neighbour. your sister will email the eulogy from australia & it is you who will have to swallow down every last fragment of terror & anxiety as you read it from the pulpit to a dozen or so distant relatives, most of whom will fail to acknowledge you with any warmth whatsoever.

- you will start to feel closer to & less afraid of death & will start referring to death as *the other side*. you will start to look forward to being on the other side.

SECTION 2

*what you can expect now you are fully transitioned to adulthood!*

- in this exciting new phase of your life you will suddenly find you need to eat less & will apply yourself to drinking more.

- you will sleep more &, liberatingly, care less (about pretty much everything).

- you will accept that the entire world may end on your watch & apart from separating your plastics from your papers, there is really little else you can do.

- you will continue drinking & placing your empties in the correct bin, but when the correct bin is full you will place them in whichever bin you feel like placing them in. yes, sometimes even the green bin.

- there is a strong possibility menopause will be an absolute cunt.

- you will buy a fan, stay hydrated, try bio-identical hormone therapy, eat yams & gulp down black cohosh like it was going out of fashion. none of it will help in any way whatsoever.

- you will read a lot about mindfulness. if you wanted to, you could be nicer to people.

- at the same time you are now very tired of always being nice to people, & will admit to a certain frisson of excitement when at the self checkout at the supermarket you ask the supervisor where the plastic bags are kept & when she points at the feet of another customer (who may, unknowingly, be carrying the coronavirus) you will say (out loud) *what a stupid fucking place to keep them.* you will be surprised at how deliciously liberating it feels to say precisely what you are thinking.

- you will imagine you'd have been in your 80s before you started shouting at young people on skateboards on the pavement, but in fact here it is in your fifties. the feeling is intoxicating. no wonder old people love doing this so much.

- you will eat as many hot chips dipped in aioli as your heart desires but continue to avoid corn & nuts (despite the latest research indicating that corn & nuts are no longer contraindicated in the management of your diverticulitis).

## SECTION 3

*what of the future?*

- keeping your bar of expectation low is key to a happy & fulfilling life. the reality is there is very little to look forward to apart from the Dan Murphy emails that will land in your inbox weekly asking you to rate your recent purchase of twelve bottles of *Trois Clefs, Côtes du Rhône* & you will feel flattered Dan cares so much about your opinion.

- you will bulk buy items that are on special in the supermarket. this will pay off when the pandemic comes & while people are fighting over toilet rolls in the aisles, you, rather smugly, will use several more squares per wipe than is reasonable. you will luxuriate in this feeling of pandemic superiority.

- you will move to a sleepy village by the sea because life is cheaper & quieter (or so you thought till you discovered a surprising number of residents seem to blow their leaves & chainsaw trees from dawn to fucking dusk).

- on reading an interview with martin scorsese you will discover a very artistic movie streaming service called www.mubi.com & you will subscribe. the movies will be in turkish, chinese, french &, very often, serbian. you will tell everyone of this extraordinary treasure trove of art-house movies you have discovered via martin (as though he were your friend) though you will watch hardly any of them because at the end of the day, netflix does offer more in terms of true entertainment.

- you will read the latest research on why it's important to drink less booze & how this may extend your life by another two years. you will wonder who would want to extend their life by two years if they're not drinking.

## CONCLUSION

now you have transitioned to adulthood, we hope you will come to the very comforting conclusion that all that shit you spent fifty years worrying about doesn't matter in the slightest because, actually, nothing matters in the slightest.

you will now become acutely aware that for some time you believed your contribution to the world was important. do not worry, we have all been deluded in this way at one time or another.

this realisation is a normal, healthy part of transitioning to adulthood.

you will also realise that most of your life has been spent living a lie. it is important to note there is no *one-lie-fits-all*—everyone's lie is different. try to resist comparing your lies with other people's (although this manual accepts that this will be especially difficult if you are still using facebook, twitter or instagram).

all of us here at *transitioning to adulthood—a manual for women in their fifties!* wish you good health & inappropriate outbursts on your very individual road ahead. for daily inspiration download our app & go into the draw to win a year's supply of *Trois Clefs, Côtes du Rhône*—& remember, if you find a lower price on any of Dan Murphy's wines, they'll beat it on the spot. hurry, offer may end soon.

# sex in bunnings

*Interviewer: and why do you love him in particular?*

because after twenty-five years of marriage when i told him last
night i dreamt we were having sex in bunnings, his first question
was, *which aisle?*

because his toilet reading is made up of *The Atheist Manifesto, Un
Portrait Logique et Moral de la Haine,* and *How To Argue with a
Racist*

because his bookmarks are delicate fragments of quilted three ply

because he keeps a second iPad in the toilet for things that may
need to be googled as a matter of urgency

because a week after we met he said he wanted to grow old with
me

because when i'm feeling down he tells me a french joke translated
into english even though 'french' & 'joke' in the same sentence is
oxymoronic

because he refuses to eat cheese casually referred to as parmesan
unless it comes from the actual, you know, province of parma

because one time i caught him staring longingly at the $1 hot dog
sign at ikea

because he spends his time thinking about the world's dwindling
energy resources

because when we walk past the clothing store *diesel* he quietly remarks how one day they may have to change their name to *solar*, maybe even *wind*

because he promised when i grew frail, he would wipe my arse for me—without disgust

because when he says this he punctuates the air with his forefinger to emphasise the first syllables of *with*out & *dis*gust

because whenever i ask if he heard what i just said he always says yes

because when pressed on the above he will confess he didn't actually hear what i said, but answered yes because the probability of this being the correct answer has a statistical weighting of 78–93% (+/– 5% margin of error)

because in winter he fills four hot-water bottles & spaces them evenly down my side of the bed

because when i come home with a new mascara he always asks why i didn't buy two

because every time he stares off into the distance, i ask if it's about the $1 hotdog again

because when i told him i was leaving i feared he might die

because when i left he almost did.

## what started as a haiku turned into this

i        don't    know    if      a

door    has      ever    slammed          shut    in

your    heart    but     it      makes

(a very loud fucking bang).

# thou shalt not wank

criticise me if you like for speaking about my daughters, but they are the centre of my life. my wife is the centre of my life. my widowed mother is the centre of my life *the lord is my shepherd my staffers shall not wank (especially on the desks of female ministers).*

but my wife jenni & i spoke last night & she told me i have to think about this as a father first & what would i want to happen if it were our girls *and yea though i walk through the valley of the shadow of alleged rape i will not step outside my office in order to acknowledge the women who marched on my doorstep (and nor, for that matter, will my so-called minister for women).*

but let us not forget, not far from here, such marches, even now are being met with bullets, but not here in this country, mr speaker. *& lo! the women of the land did cheer when they were not gunned down for exercising their right to peaceful protest.*

but i acknowledge that many australians, especially women, believe that i have not heard them, and that greatly distresses me *however i for one will fear no women, for the law & the boys club art with me & my ministerial staff doth protect me.*

of course women put up with this rubbish & this crap for their entire lives & *they will certainly continue to fear evil* for no single individual can be watched, on every single inch of parliament house, every second of the day. *& our deputy prime minister michael mccormack doth restore my soul & lead us in the direction of righteousness* as he commits to spending an 'hour or two' in empathy training because, as he says, if we can learn from an expert on how to not only be better ourselves but how to call out others for it, then this is a very good thing.

but all of this has been shocking. it is shameful & i am disgusted. of course we all know that blokes don't get it right all the time, but what matters is that we're desperately trying to. *surely goodness & mercy shall follow parliamentarians all the days of their lives.*

today, australian women, but australians more broadly, need to know that this place has heard them & that i have heard them. my daughters motivate me every day on this issue & to them i say to you, girls, i will not let you down (*even though my cup runneth over with lies & my empathy dehydrated long before the drought*).

*let us pray,*

scott morrison, who art in hillsong, hallowed be
thy name. thy kingdom come, thy will be done in
parliament as it is in your own version of heaven.
give us this day, our daily *sex scandal & forgive us
our trespasses as we rarely forgive those who have
trespassed against us.*

*& lead us not into temptation,* (though when we have
been, let the record state it is always the woman's
fault), *but deliver us from the evil accusation of rape
in the office a few doors down the corridor from thy
own.*

dear lord, we are gathered here today *to get our liberal
house in order,* lest our government fall into minority
*& parliament house no longer remains the kingdom,
the white male power & the glory forever & ever.
amen.*

The footage of a liberal party staffer masturbating on
a female minister's desk, the alleged rape of a staffer on a
minister's couch in parliament house & the complete lack
of empathy, understanding & hypocrisy of our Australian
hillsong prime minister made my blood boil hotter than
the planet. This found poem, 'thou shalt not wank' (made
mostly from scott morrison quotes), is the result of my anger.
Non-italicised lines are direct quotes from Scott Morrison's
utterances; italics indicate my rage.

# fifty-six winters after the arse slap

*whenever any of us left a door open at home, my father would yell, 'were you born in a fucking field?' i was the only one in my family who could confidently reply yes.*

scotland.

october.

2018.

frost.

low sky.

i.

i stand outside the field, close my eyes try to project the hand-me-down memories onto the big screen of my imagination—the doctor cantering across this same field; the doctor dismounting at the bothy door; the doctor running inside to discover me already arse-slapped & in the world courtesy of my grandmother—the first baby she's ever delivered & not a single youtube tutorial in sight.

ii.

the gate's hinges are furred with rust, its rotting posts wobble, the *please close the gate* sign hangs by a thread. mum goes first, places her left foot tentatively on the gate's first rung, steadies a moment before wheeching her right leg over the top. the rest of her body follows. she lands, despite her 77 years, like an elite athlete in the field on the other side.

iii.

i go next; step precariously onto the first rung. i too wheech my right leg—*take a photo of me* i shout holding my wheech mid-air trying to make it look as though i were innocently caught on camera, evidence to post later of me living my best life (*social media, what have you done to me?*).

iv.

fifty-six winters after the arse slap the bothy lies derelict, lost in a forest of brambles. once fragile boy-weeds have morphed into tall, overpowering men. previously shy girl-thistles in soft purple crowns have sprouted into exhausted women, their slim necks broken, heads flailing backwards, mouths gaping silently towards the sky. tiny crab apples dangle through the rafters like miniature baubles on a deprived christmas tree. sparrows nest in what's left of the eaves.

v.

mum leans into the brambles, has had a lifetime of this, knows exactly where to place her

shoulder to avoid the worst of the thorns. she
stands on her tiptoes, picks the brambles from
up on high [caution: never pick brambles from the
bottom of a bush, a dog may have pished on them].
she holds them in her out-stretched hand. ink
from their pierced membranes stain the plump
pink of her palm & trickles through her love-
line like a river of mascara.

vi.

i take three of the berries offered; dense &
glowing, their soft bulge fills my mouth &
reminds me of poet liz lochhead's *persimmons*.
i splat each bramble between my hard palate &
my tongue. memories wash down the soft chute
of my throat, fill me like a contrast dye on a
CT scan highlighting the internal injury of my
past, the blockages of my present, the chronic
inflammation of my days ahead.

# in the air bnb where you have taken yourself & the wrung-out swimsuit of your sorrow

peel off the tired pyjama pants of your anguish. let the king size doona of your grief engulf you in the single bed not meant for this much sadness. breathe what's left of you into your elasticated waistband that lets you expand & contract into who you need to be. do not attempt to extinguish the flames of your emptiness with a carpet beater. instead dampen them with the soft shower of your garden hose or the mini fire extinguisher in the air bnb where you have taken yourself & the wrung-out swimsuit of your sorrow wrapped tightly in the bath towel of your despair. familiarise yourself with the exits closest to you. the sign on the wall reads *in case of emergency call this number.* you call this number. no one tells you your call is important to them. you are not placed in a queue. the operator asks where you are. you tell her you are in a brown field; that it is very far away; that it is strangely familiar to you. you tell her there are many cows but no grass; that the water trough is empty; that the herd is staring out across the winding road rising & falling over distant hills hoping the farmer's tractor will appear loaded with feed. the operator asks if there is anything else. you tell her yes, each time a vehicle passes without stopping the cows' sad lowing adds another leaf to the mille-feuille of your sadness; that the wind is barrelling in from the west casting off sheets of topsoil like chiffon scarves from the heads of bald women declared cancer free; that the topsoil is magic-carpeting its way through the sky, crop dusting cities not used to the earth's dried blood settling on pavements, thick like paprika thrown as punishment from the heavy hand of a hungarian god. the operator asks again if there is anything else. you tell her you cannot think of anything. she offers you a few kind words which you may or may not be able to hear. she tells you if you cannot hear the words today you may ring again tomorrow. you select end call, step through the exit closest to you, lick your finger & hold it to the wind. the fine pollen of your grief settles on its tip. you breathe into your elasticated waistband, stare out across the winding road rising & falling over distant hills. you pray for rain. for an end to the lowing.

**give**

**me**

**a**

**poem**

with a · · · dotted line tattooed across
its throat saying CUT HERE
       give

me a poem with its knickers at its
its ankles skirt hoiked up around
its waist running bare-arsed through
the shitstorm of this world give

       me a

poem that smokes two fags simul-
taneously & sucks on a bottle of
jack give me a

poem that gorges on transfats &
kale & lives in perfect harmony
with its cunt-radictions give

me          a          poem

that sings through the bedlam of the
asylum & the solitary confinement of
this fucking jail

    gi
    ve m
    e a po
    em

with a pierced tongue & moist
cleavage & hot pants so short it must
have been fucking asking for it give
me

                         a poem

that plays the violin backwards &
rachmaninoff's 5th on a broken
piano left out in the rain

        g  i  v  e

me a poem that gives zero fucks shaves
its head & never speaks latin—ever.

        gi        ve
        me       a
        p        oem

that unfurls me bloated from the
sodden carpet of myself

°give  me  a  poe m°

that waterboards me till i'm lifeless &
drowning in love


    gi
    ve
    me
    ap
    oe
    m

that douses me in vinegar

    givemeapoem

          that


     rolls


        me


            in


     salt.

# acknowledgements

I am deeply indebted to the entire team at Wakefield Press (in particular the brilliant Julia Beaven & Michael Bollen) who seem to see whatever it is I am trying to say in these pages and who embrace the work in a way that floors me with gratitude with every book we do together.

A huge thanks goes to my wee maw who's encouragement knows no bounds and who has never faltered in her belief that I should always strive to spend my life doing precisely what I love.

Thank you to my family for somehow always loving what I do—I'm looking at you Alexandra, Izzy, Andrew, Fiona & Bronwyn.

A massive thankyou to anyone who has ever commented on a poem, liked or shared a post or bought a book. Thank you to Kri, who sends me cards addressed to 'The Poet' in the hope that the postman will notice and maybe one day buy a book. God loves a trier. I am grateful to you all.

Some of these poems were first published in the following magazines, anthologies & websites: *The Moth*, Red Room Poetry, Art Gallery of New South Wales, *Pink Cover Zine*, *Gitanjali and Beyond*, *Abridged*, *One Hand Clapping*, *Verity La*, *Borderless: A transnational anthology of feminist poetry*.

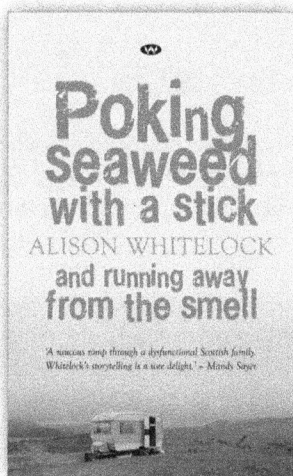

Poking
seaweed
with a stick
ALISON WHITELOCK
and running away
from the smell

*A raucous romp through a dysfunctional Scottish family.
Whitelock's storytelling is a wee delight.'* – Mindy Sayer

'Whitelock is Bukowski with a Glaswegian
accent and more wardrobe. She is Sharon Olds
with better manners.' – MARK TREDINNICK

and my heart
crumples
like a
coke can

ali whitelock

'Tremendously witty and deeply moving poetry.'
– MELANIE TAIT

the lactic acid
in the calves of
your despair

ali whitelock

Wakefield Press is an independent publishing and
distribution company based in Adelaide, South Australia.
We love good stories and publish beautiful books.
To see our full range of books, please visit our website at
www.wakefieldpress.com.au
where all titles are available for purchase.
To keep up with our latest releases, news and events,
subscribe to our monthly newsletter.

Find us!

Facebook: www.facebook.com/wakefield.press
Twitter: www.twitter.com/wakefieldpress
Instagram: www.instagram.com/wakefieldpress

www.ingramcontent.com/pod-product-compliance
Lightning Source LLC
Chambersburg PA
CBHW022159080426
42734CB00006B/498